Contents

The sports buzz 4

Ancient sports 6

Deadly sports 8

Early ball games 10

Rules and regulations 12

A changing world 14

Prejudice in sport 16

Sport on the screen 18

Sport for everyone 20

Money and fame 22

Extreme sports 24

Rising to the challenge 26

Key dates 28

Glossary 30

Find out more.. 31

Index 32

Historical time is divided into two major periods. BC is short for "before Christ" – that is, the time before the Christian religion began. This is the time up to the year 1 BC. AD is short for "Anno Domini". This is Latin for "in the year of our Lord", meaning the time from the year 1 BC to the present. For example, when the calendar says the year is AD 1000, it is 1000 years after the year 1 BC. The abbreviation *c.* stands for *circa*, which is Latin for "around".

Any words appearing in the text in bold, **like this**, are explained in the glossary.

The sports buzz

People enjoy sport for many different reasons: to get fit, compete, break records, feel part of a team, and to make money. Some people play just for fun!

Ever-changing

Sport itself has changed a lot through time. Gradually new sports appeared and the first rules were made. We will see how sport grew to be a common **leisure** activity, as well as a money-making industry. Other developments have influenced sport. New technology has provided better equipment, such as rackets and balls. International competitions only became possible when transport improved. When there were no aircraft or fast boats, sportspeople could not travel overseas. Now spectators jet all over the world to see competitions.

Determined

Over the centuries, one thing has not changed – to be successful in sport, people must practise often, and hard! Throughout history, people have worked hard to stand out from the crowd as sport stars. Determined to win, they give most of their time to their sport.

Pictures from ancient tombs show that about 4000 years ago ordinary Egyptians did many of the sports we enjoy today, from wrestling to high jumps.

TIMELINE HISTORY

SPORT

From Ancient Olympics to the Champions League

Liz Miles

www.raintreepublishers.co.uk
Visit our website to find out more information about Raintree books.

To order:

☎ Phone 0845 6044371

🖨 Fax +44 (0) 1865 312263

💻 Email myorders@raintreepublishers.co.uk

Customers from outside the UK please telephone +44 1865 312262

Raintree is an imprint of Capstone Global Library Limited, a company incorporated in England and Wales having its registered office at 7 Pilgrim Street, London, EC4V 6LB – Registered company number: 6695582

Edited by Louise Galpine and Diyan Leake
Designed by Richard Parker
Original illustrations © Capstone Global Library Ltd 2011
Illustrated by Jeff Edwards
Picture research by Hannah Taylor
Originated by Dot Gradations Ltd
Printed and bound in China by CTPS

ISBN 978 0 431 02554 4 (hardback)
14 13 12 11 10
10 9 8 7 6 5 4 3 2 1

ISBN 978 0 431 02562 9 (paperback)
15 14 13 12 11
10 9 8 7 6 5 4 3 2 1

British Library Cataloguing in Publication Data
Miles, Liz. – Sport : from ancient Olympics to the Champions League. – (Timeline history)
796'.09-dc22
A full catalogue record for this book is available from the British Library.

Acknowledgements
We would like to thank the following for permission to reproduce photographs: Alamy Images pp. **10** top (© Lordprice Collection), **12** top (© Imagepast), **26** (© NearTheCoast. com); Bishop Museum Archive p. **13**; Corbis pp. **7** top (Amit Dey), **8** (Atlantide Phototravel), **16** bottom (Bettmann), **18** top (Bettmann), **20** bottom (Xinhua Press/Zhang Yanhui), **22** top (Bettmann), **22** bottom (Leo Mason), **25** (epa/Kerim Okten); Getty Images pp. **5** (AFP Photo/Fabrice Coffrini), **10** bottom (AFP Photo/Luis Acosta), **12** bottom (The Bridgeman Art Library), **14** (Transcendental Graphics/Mark Rucker), **15** bottom (Popperfoto), **16** top (Diamond Images/Kidwiler Collection), **17**, **18** bottom (Hulton Archive), **19** (Diamond Images/Kidwiler Collection), **20** top (Popperfoto), **21** Express/Clive Limpkin), **24** bottom (AFP Photo/Joe Klamar), **27** (Jasper Juinen); Motoring Picture Library p. **15** top; Photolibrary pp. **6** (Walter Bibikow), **7** bottom (View Stock), **11** (North Wind Pictures); Rex Features p. **24** top (KPA/ Zuma); The Advertising Archives p. **23**; The Art Archive pp. **4** (Dagli Orti), **9** top, **9** bottom (Dagli Orti).

Cover photograph of Barcelona football team celebrating winning the UEFA Champions League in Rome, Italy in 2009, reproduced with permission of Getty Images (Alex Livesey).

Every effort has been made to contact copyright holders of material reproduced in this book. Any omissions will be rectified in subsequent printings if notice is given to the publisher.

Disclaimer

Jamaican sprinter Usain Bolt broke world records at the 2009 World Athletics Championships in Berlin, Germany.

Timelines

The information in this book is on a timeline. A timeline shows you events from history in the order they happened. The big timeline in the middle of each page gives you details of a certain time in history (see below).

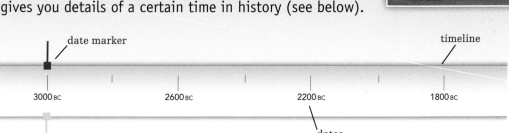

date marker

timeline

3000 BC   2600 BC   2200 BC   1800 BC

dates

Some dates are exact. For example, the first modern Olympic Games were held in 1896. Others are more general because there were no written records of an event or it took place over a period of time. The smaller timeline at the bottom of each page shows you how the page you are reading fits into history as a whole. You will read about sports from all around the world. Each entry on the main timeline is in a different colour. This colour shows you which continent the information is about. The map below shows you how this colour coding works. Pale green indicates events that took place on more than one continent or worldwide.

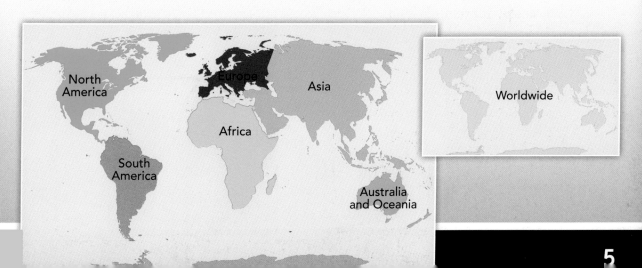

North America

Europe

Asia

Worldwide

Africa

South America

Australia and Oceania

Ancient sports

In **prehistoric** times, people spent most of their time hunting for food. But they may have enjoyed the thrill of running and swimming, too. The oldest evidence of sport comes from the first **civilizations**, such as those of the ancient Greeks and Egyptians.

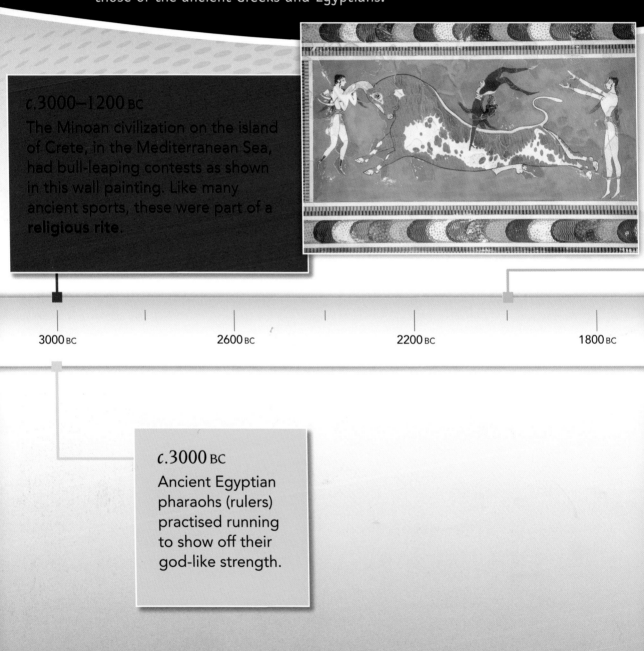

*c.*3000–1200 BC
The Minoan civilization on the island of Crete, in the Mediterranean Sea, had bull-leaping contests as shown in this wall painting. Like many ancient sports, these were part of a **religious rite**.

3000 BC   2600 BC   2200 BC   1800 BC

*c.*3000 BC
Ancient Egyptian pharaohs (rulers) practised running to show off their god-like strength.

c.2000 BC

Kabaddi was first played in India. It is like a mix of wrestling and rugby where players make raids on the other team while holding their breath.

600 BC

Persian soldiers played the first recorded game of polo. They played on horseback with a stick and a ball. Some say the ball was the head of an enemy soldier.

1400 BC   1000 BC   600 BC

776 BC   ANCIENT OLYMPICS

The first ancient Olympic Games were held in Olympia, Greece in honour of the Greek god Zeus. The first Olympics had one event – a men's sprint of nearly 200 metres (219 yards), as painted on this vase. Later, it included the discus, javelin, and weight-lifting. The women had separate games in honour of the goddess Hera.

Deadly sports

As populations grew in cities in Europe and Asia, bigger crowds gathered to watch sport. Dangerous sports were very popular. People began to bet money on who might win. Prizes, such as cash, were often given to the winning athletes.

AD 39–92

An ancient Chinese book (the *Han Shu*) talks about a form of martial arts in "Six Chapters of Hand Fighting".

AD 320–1200

Some sports were more dangerous for animals than for people. During this period fights between rams (male sheep) were popular in India. People bet on which animal might win.

AD 1   AD 250   AD 500

AD 192   DEATH AND DEFEAT

Chariot racing was at its most popular in ancient Rome. Up to 250,000 people watched in the vast Circus Maximus arena. In a crash, charioteers often got caught in the horses' reins and were dragged along the ground. They often died. Many charioteers were **slaves** who hoped to win enough money to buy their freedom.

1185–1233

Fearsome Japanese fighters called samurai practised sword fighting, horse-riding, and archery. They believed that it was better to die than be defeated.

AD 750   AD 1000   AD 1250

AD 1100s

In Britain and France, knights practised their fighting skills in jousting tournaments.

Early ball games

All kinds of ball games were played around the world. They were without rules and often dangerous. The balls were made from any materials that were available. Rubber plants to make bouncing balls only grew in certain parts of the world.

1314

Football was banned in a part of London because of the trouble it caused. "Mob football" (as it was called) had few rules and was played by noisy crowds on the streets.

| 1300 | 1325 | 1350 | 1375 | 1400 |

1325–1521

The Aztecs forced their prisoners of war to play a game called tlachtli. Teams competed to get a rubber ball through a stone ring.

1400s

Golf began to be played in Scotland, the players hitting their feather-filled ball into a series of holes over hilly land.

1492

When Christopher Columbus landed in the West Indies, he witnessed the Tainos people playing a two-team game on a clay court called a batey. A rubber ball had to be kept in the air by hitting it with any part of the body except the hands.

1425   1450   1475   1500

1400s NATIVE AMERICAN GAMES

Many Native American peoples played stick and ball games similar to today's **lacrosse**. Iroquois Native Americans played baggataway. They used a single stick with a triangular net to throw and catch a ball made of bone or rock.

Rules and regulations

By the 1500s, some sports became less rough in the West. Rules were agreed upon and recorded. By 1800, there were many **sedate** sports, including cricket, billiards, and bowls. In the East, sports were often still linked to ceremonies. Some sports were only for the very rich.

1526–1857

On special occasions, rulers in India enjoyed watching fights between elephants. The sport was not for ordinary common people.

1500   1550   1600   1650

1599

The first rules for an early form of tennis were published. This painting shows tennis being played in Italy in the 1700s.

c.1700

A popular form of **kung fu** developed in China, called wing chun (which means "eternal spring time"). A legend says that it is named after a woman who used this style of fighting to beat a warlord.

1744

Rules for cricket were written down. Some gentlemen in London felt it was impossible to play cricket fairly without any common rules. Their first "Laws of Cricket" still form the basis of cricket today.

1700   1750   1800

1779

The British explorer Captain Cook sailed to Hawaii. One of his officers wrote in his journal how amazed he was at the skills of surfers on the rocky shorelines of Hawaii.

A changing world

By the 1800s, the effects of the **Industrial Revolution** changed the world of sport. Improved transport, such as steamships and steam trains, led to the first county, national, and world championships. Growing populations in cities turned to sport for fun. Motor racing was made possible by the invention of the **engine**.

1845

The first American baseball teams and clubs formed in towns and cities. In 1869, the first **professional** team was formed: the Cincinnati Red Stockings (right).

1840   1850   1860   1870

1876

The rules of badminton were written down, based on how the game was played in Poona, India. Badminton clubs began to form in the United States and Europe.

1877

The England cricket team travelled by steamboat to Melbourne, Australia for the first cricket Test match. Australia won by 45 runs.

1883

The first rugby Home Nations Championship was held. It is said that rugby was invented when a football player at Rugby School in Warwickshire, England, picked up the ball and ran with it. American football soon grew out of a mix of rugby and Association football (soccer).

1895

The first organized motor race took place on roads in France.

1880   1890   1900

1896

Crowds and athletes travelled to the first modern Olympic Games. It was held in Athens, Greece.

Prejudice in sport

By the 1920s female athletes proved that they had the strength and skill to do what had been "men only" sports. However, Africans and African Americans were still excluded because of **racial prejudice**.

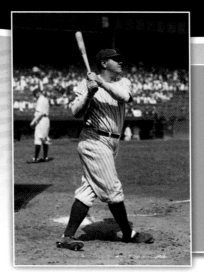

1930
The first football **World Cup** match was hosted by Uruguay. Uruguay won the final against Argentina, 4–2.

1930
One of the first ever sport superstars, baseball player George Herman Ruth ("Babe Ruth"), was earning $80,000 a year by 1930.

1920   1925   1930   1935

1936
African Americans Louise Stokes (back row, 3rd from left) and Tidye Pickett (back row, 1st on right) were finally allowed to compete as relay runners in the Olympic Games. In 1932, racial prejudice had caused them to be excluded from the games.

1936

Hitler's Nazi Germany was host to the Olympic Games in Berlin. Hitler believed that only white-skinned, blue-eyed, fair-haired people could achieve highly in sport. He was proved wrong when African American Jesse Owens won four gold medals at the Games.

1940

1945

1950

1940s SEGREGATION

Around the world, **segregation** in sport was still common. In the United States, African-American sports people were usually only allowed to enter "black only" sports events or teams. In 1947, Jackie Robinson was the first African-American baseball player to play in the US Majors League since 1889.

present day

Sport on the screen

The invention of television allowed more people to watch sport. It also brought **advertising** and **sponsorship** so that sports teams and organizations could raise money. Sports people could make a living with their skills.

1950s

Basketball player Bob Cousy (wearing number 14, right) was in great demand and insisted on a huge salary before agreeing to play for the Boston Celtics.

| 1950 | 1951 | 1952 | 1953 | 1954 |

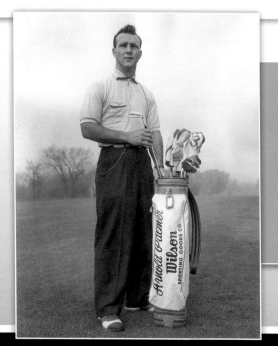

1953

US golfer Arnold Palmer gained a big salary from prizes and advertising. Here he poses for a sports equipment advert.

1958 TV SPORT

About 45 million viewers watched the nail-biting US National Football League (NFL) Championship Game on television. The Baltimore Colts defeated the New York Giants 23–17 during overtime. The NFL Championship Game was the first **professional** American football game to draw a big TV audience. The Colts–Giants game became known as "The Greatest Game Ever Played" and made the sport very popular.

1955   1956   1957   1958

1954

British athlete Roger Bannister was the first to run a mile in under 4 minutes.

1956

At the Australian Olympics, a match between the Hungary and **USSR** water polo teams became violent – a month earlier the USSR had invaded Hungary.

Sport for everyone

Desegregation in public schools and public organizations in the United States began to be **enforced** in 1954. Protests against continuing racism in sport and **apartheid** in South Africa grew. Soon many more Africans began to win championships. The Paralympics allowed people with disabilities to compete internationally.

1960

The Ethiopian runner Abebe Bikila was the winner of the Olympic marathon. As a last-minute replacement for a team-mate, Bikila had no comfortable shoes so he ran barefoot.

1960   1961   1962   1963   1964

1960   PARALYMPICS

The first Paralympic Games were held in Rome, Italy. They involved 400 athletes with **spinal cord** injuries. The athletes competed in eight sports, including fencing, field events, and table tennis. Today, people with all kinds of disabilities compete in the Paralympics. South African sprinter Oscar Pritorius won gold in the 2008 Paralympics (right).

1965

The American League All-Star baseball game was to be played in the city of New Orleans. But when African-American players were turned away from some restaurants, the players protested. The event was moved to another American city, Houston.

1965 | 1966 | 1967 | 1968

1965

The first Pan-African Games (now called the All-Africa Games) were held in Congo. People in many countries were united against apartheid. Anti-apartheid protestors (right) demonstrated when white South African cricketers came to London.

Money and fame

Money earned from prizes and sponsors turned **amateur** champions into **professional** sports stars. Some greedy athletes broke the rules and took drugs to help them win. But most just practised hard.

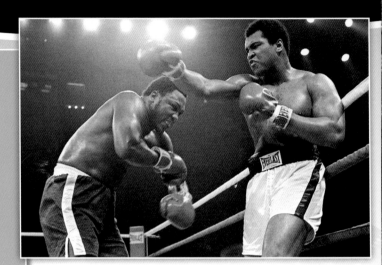

1975

A match called the "Thrilla in Manila" took place in the Philippines, between the US heavyweight boxers Muhammad Ali (on the right) and Joe Frazier. Ali won, but the battle affected the health of both fighters.

| 1970 | 1972 | 1974 | 1976 | 1978 | 1980 |

1976

In Canada, a 14-year-old Romanian, Nadia Elena Comăneci, was the first ever gymnast to get the top score of 10 in the Olympic Games.

MICHAEL JORDAN 1
ISAAC NEWTON 0

1985

US basketball superstar Michael Jordan received $2.5 million from sportswear-makers Nike, so that they could make a new line of trainers called Nike Air Jordan.

1982   1984   1986   1988   1990

1988 DOPING

Canadian sprinter Ben Johnson was found guilty of taking drugs at the Olympics in Seoul, South Korea, and his gold medal was taken away. Other sports stars took drugs to make them perform better. This is called "doping". Scientists found new ways of testing athletes for these drugs.

Extreme sports

Sport has become bigger and faster, and it attracts vast sums of money. New and dangerous sports, known as extreme sports, have been developed. New drugs have been invented that enhance an athlete's performance. Banned drugs are becoming harder to detect.

1990s BIG WAVES

The latest form of extreme surfing is "tow-in surfing". A person on a powered watercraft tows the surfer out to where the biggest, 12-metre (40-foot) waves are.

1990   1994   1998

1998

Snowboarding became a sport at the Winter Olympics in Japan. Olympic snowboarding is completed on a prepared course.

2004

Major League Baseball began to test players for banned drugs during the sports season.

2007
US basketball superstar LeBron James came top of the list of the world's richest under-25-year-olds. From 2006 to 2007 he earned $27 million.

2002

2006

2010

2008
At the Beijing Olympics in China, US swimmer Michael Phelps won eight gold medals – the most anyone has won at an Olympic Games.

2008
The UEFA Champions League (football's European Cup) final in Russia was played between two British teams for the first time. Manchester United beat Chelsea in an exciting penalty shootout (6–5).

Rising to the challenge

Slow down, please!

Some people are fed-up with speed-driven sports, when life itself is so fast and tiring. Slow sports offer an alternative. The winner of a slow bicycle race is the person who takes the longest to finish the course!

The cyclist at the front is losing this slow bicycle race!

Athletes love their sport and will overcome all kinds of challenges to take part. Sports people also help others to overcome difficulties, too. Many sports events raise money for charities.

There is a lot of money to be made in sport, but you don't need much to enjoy it. The most popular sport in the world to watch and play is football. To play it you only really need a cheap ball and some friends!

An inspiration

In 1998 US racing cyclist Lance Armstrong returned to cycling after suffering from cancer. He went on to win the Tour de France cycling competition seven times. He then retired for a while but was back again in 2009. He races to raise money to help and to inspire cancer sufferers.

Lance Armstrong (at the front) and his teammates cycled up the steep route of the Tour de France in 2009.

Key dates

c.3000 BC
Ancient Egyptian pharaohs practise running to show off their god-like strength.

776 BC
The first ancient Olympic Games are held in Olympia, Greece.

AD 192
Chariot racing is at its most popular in ancient Rome.

1325–1521
The Aztecs force their prisoners of war to play tlachtli. Teams compete to get a rubber ball through a stone ring.

1400s
Golf begins to be played in Scotland.

c.1700
A popular form of **kung fu** develops in China, called wing chun (which means "eternal spring time").

1744
The rules for cricket are written down.

1845
The first American baseball teams and clubs are formed in towns and cities.

1896
Crowds and athletes travel to the first modern Olympic Games in Athens, Greece.

1940s
Around the world, **segregation** in sport is still common.

1958
About 45 million viewers watch the US National Football League Championship Game on television.

1960
The Ethiopian runner Abebe Bikila runs barefoot to become the winner of the Olympic marathon.

1965
The first Pan-African Games are held in Congo.

1975
A match called the "Thrilla in Manila" takes place between US heavyweight boxers Muhammad Ali and Joe Frazier.

1988
Canadian sprinter Ben Johnson is found guilty of taking drugs at the Olympics in Seoul, South Korea, and his gold medal is taken away.

1998
Snowboarding becomes a sport at the Winter Olympics in Japan.

2008
At the Beijing Olympics in China, US swimmer Michael Phelps wins eight gold medals.

Glossary

advertising display of a product on television or on posters to help sell it

amateur someone who does a sport for a hobby, not a job. Amateur sportspeople do not get paid for their skills.

apartheid system of separating whites and non-whites in South Africa. Apartheid meant the non-whites were treated unfairly.

civilization particular society or culture at a particular period of time

desegregation encouraging people to do everything together, no matter what their skin colour is

enforce force something to happen by law

engine machine that burns fuel to turn energy into movement

Industrial Revolution period from 1750 to 1850 when items started to be made in factories by machine

kung fu form of self-defence using kicks and punches. Kung fu is a martial art, similar to karate.

lacrosse game in which players catch a hard ball in a net on a stick

leisure enjoyment, not at work

prehistoric before records were written down in any way

professional someone who does something as a job, not a hobby

racial prejudice belief that a person's skill or talent depends on that person's race

religious rite ceremony linked to religious beliefs. Many sports began as religious rites.

sedate calm and unhurried

segregation separating people according to the colour of their skin

slave servant who is not paid, but owned

spinal cord nerve cells in the backbone that connect much of the body to the brain. People with bad spinal cord injuries may not be able to walk.

sponsorship giving money to help someone do something. Sponsorship money helps sports people to buy equipment.

USSR Union of Soviet Socialist Republics, which later split into the Russian Federation and other countries

World Cup four-yearly football tournament

Find out more

Books

Athletics **(Inside Sport series)**, Clive Gifford (Wayland, 2010)

Back on the Beam **(Sport Stories series)**, Eric Stevens (Raintree, 2010)

Football Shootout **(Sport Stories series)**, Bob Temple (Raintree, 2010)

Getting into Surfing, Luke and Damien Davis (Nelson Thornes, 2008)

Guinness World Records 2010 (Guinness World Records Ltd, 2010)

Half-pipe Prize **(Sport Stories series)**, Eric Stevens (Raintree, 2010)

Sport Files series (Raintree, 2009)

Welcome to the Ancient Olympics!, Jane Bingham (Raintree, 2007)

Websites

Pick up some hot tips from top sport stars:

news.bbc.co.uk/sport1/hi/academy/default.stm

On the Ancient Olympics:

www.perseus.tufts.edu/Olympics/

About the big sports charity, Sport Relief:

www.sportrelief.com

There is a list of sports museums to visit at:

www.sportsmuseums.co.uk/museums.htm

Index

advertising and
sponsorship 18
African Americans 16,
17, 21
American football 15, 19
animal contests 8, 12
apartheid 20, 21
archery 9
Aztecs 10

badminton 14
baggataway 11
ball games, early 10–11
baseball 14, 16, 17, 21, 24
basketball 18, 23, 25
batey 11
betting 8
boxing 22
Britain 9, 10, 11, 13, 15, 19
bull-leaping 6

chariot racing 8
charity work 27
China 8, 13
cricket 13, 14, 21
cycling 26, 27

dangerous sports 8–9
disabilities, people with 20
discus 7
drugs 23, 24

Egypt 4, 6
extreme sports 24–5

female athletes 7, 16, 22
fencing 20
football 10, 15, 16, 19, 25
France 9

golf 11, 18
Greece 7, 15
gymnastics 22

Hawaii 13
horse-riding 9

India 7, 8, 12, 18

Japan 9
javelin 7
jousting 9

kabaddi 7
kung fu 13

lacrosse 11

marathons 20
martial arts 8, 13
Minoan civilization 6
motor racing 15

Native Americans 11

Olympic Games 5, 7, 15, 16,
17, 19, 20, 22, 23, 25

Pan-African Games 21
Paralympic Games 20
Persia 7
polo 7

racial prejudice 16, 17,
20, 21
religious rites 6
Romans 8
rugby 15
rules and regulations 12,
13, 14
running/sprinting 5, 6, 7,
19, 20

samurai 9
segregation 17
slaves 8
slow sports 26
snowboarding 24
South Africa 20, 21
superstars 16, 18, 22–3, 25
surfing 13, 24
swimming 25
sword-fighting 9

table tennis 20
televised sport 18, 19
tennis 12
tlachtli 10

United States 14, 15, 17,
19, 20, 21

water polo 19
weight-lifting 7
West Indies 11
Winter Olympics 24